THIS IS A CARLTON BOOK

The Dog Logo and Photographs © 2005
Artlist International Inc
Text and Design copyright © 2004
Carlton Books Limited

This edition published in 2005 by
Carlton Books Ltd
A Division of the Carlton Publishing Group
20 Mortimer Street
London
W1T 3JW

A CIP catalogue for this book is available
from the British Library.

ISBN 1 84442 695 5

Project Editor: Amie McKee
Art Director: Clare Baggaley
Design: Stuart Smith
Production: Caroline Alberti

Printed and bound in Singapore

THE DOG

Artlist Collection

LITTLE **DOGS**

CARLTON
BOOKS

Yorkshire Terrier

Yorkshire Terrier

English Cocker Spaniel

Basset Hound

Miniature Schnauzer

Miniature Schnauzer

Shetland Sheepdog

Lakeland Terrier

Beagle

Maltese

Maltese

Chihuahua

Chihuahua

Boston Terrier

Papillon

Papillon

Papillon

Japanese Terrier

Kerry Blue Terrier

Cavalier King Charles Spaniel

Cavalier King Charles Spaniel

Pekingese

Pembroke Welsh Corgi

Dachshund

Dachshund

Dachshund

Poodle

Pomeranian

Jack Russell Terrier

Jack Russell Terrier

Pug

Pug

Shiba Inu

French Bulldog

French Bulldog

French Bulldog

West Highland White Terrier

West Highland White Terrier

American Cocker Spaniel

Chin